Seduce or Die

T0363114

SEDUCE OR DIE

Jon Roffe

Surpllus

Seduce or Die
Jon Roffe

Design: Brad Haylock

First edition 2018
ISBN: 978-1-922099-29-7
Edition of 300

Typeset in STF Lido and FF Bau Pro families

Surpllus
PO Box 418
Flinders Lane 8009
Victoria, Australia

www.surpllus.com

Surpllus respectfully acknowledges the people of the Woi wurrung and Boon wurrung language groups of the eastern Kulin nations as the traditional owners of the unceded lands upon which the development of this volume has principally taken place.

Surpllus #27

After seven years of bad luck, she broke the mirror.

Francis Ponge

I

Odysseus needed glasses, not earplugs — the sirens are *everywhere*.

'Body' is the name for the crucible that transmutes time into truth.

Given the glacially slow pace of human thought, we have no other choice: we must *trust in trauma*.

Human nature is read in cheek and jowl.

The Owl of Minerva, a 24-hour Korean restaurant in Toronto.

The only vernacular shared by the aristocrat and the democrat? Misanthropy.

Midway through a thought, you notice that you are *rolling your eyes at yourself*.

More worms than cans.

You drink to kill the animal in you, but it is always the demon that dies first.

Metaphor is not a capacity belonging to language but a way of reading and listening — and not a good one.

The essential truth of humanity is revealed in the fact of clumsiness.

Honesty lies in the inclination of the neck.

Only sex that makes real the difference between being and having.

Overwrought, underworked.

To each lesson its right time. Learnt too early or too late, not a few bear force enough to kill.

The true meaning of life is the meaninglessness of convalescence.

Newly minted truth is plentiful and cheap, often available only on credit.

Every child is a voodoo doll of its parents.

You learn about things by doing them too many times.

Desires, like fleas, leap from one body to the next.

What time is spent is wasted.

The misery of mere closeness.

Prominent in the library of books that will never be written: a history of the world told from the point of view of the fear of sex.

We each carry our own flat worlds around with us.

Certain hopes only deserve the name should they be stillborn.

Each death poisons the experience of every other.

The body is the staple of the mind.

'Meritocracy' — the name of a cherubic cartoon bumblebee reproduced on the label of an indefinitely long sequence of jars of industrially produced honey.

A caught lie is not a moral but a rhythmic failure.

The pen wanders to places the mind cannot.

The perennial twilight of the imagination.

Being sick is no barrier to making yourself sicker by choice.

…as if there was only *one* pain threshold!

You learn about things by doing them too many times.

Contemporary culture would be entirely bereft without italics.

The impossibility of 'staying put' ... 'put' says it all.
Don't for a second think that it's just as easy
choosing where you are.

The soul is an ass, the driver of the getaway vehicle,
an imbecilic accomplice to the crimes of the body.

Overdrunk, you one day shock your oldest friend,
she herself no stranger to that state. Nothing
frightens us more than the apparition of the thing,
there where we expect the person to be.

Plato tells us that the philosopher, unlike the
shoddy butcher, cuts reality at the joints. Despite
everything, then, we begin with the body. Before
the idea, one is before the meat — a meatphysics
precedes every metaphysics.

The ur-virus, fantasy; the ur-fantasy, the virus.

One day, the final fire will be extinguished on
some street in some city. It will be a cigarette,
no doubt — a retro throwback, a relic stolen from
a museum, or a wistful future rendition of the real
article you'll only be able to read about then. And
as the security guard cheerfully tasers its former
smoker into trembling insensibility, the last fire
will dwindle into nothing. We must imagine
Prometheus redundant.

II

A task for phenomenologists (if any are left):
to explain why the exposure to vast and empty
spaces forces us to think time.

Human beings, uniquely, can pass their sight into
tools: the tool is the extension of sight that renders
us blind. The whole of human existence falls under
this shifting penumbra.

Wittgenstein's deflationary approach to philosophical concepts finds its true field of application in
gossip. After all, when you're told 'Can you believe
she left him?', the only meaningful response is a
shrug; when you get a text message of this ilk
while in private, the body knows the appropriate
response: a meagre grunt.

Stupidity, the living paralogism.

Beware thoughts of which you are too proud: like
flies, this pride is attracted because the thought is
overripe. Be even more wary if you cannot recall
any earlier moment during which they were ripe.

Simmel was on the right track, as was Turner in his
Tenth Plague. It is true that to live in a city is to be
modified by your constant exposure to unknown
others. But the streets and stores that he invokes
are not isolated tracts of exteriority circumscribed

by a private milieu. The city is the manifestation of a pure exteriority. The city—the outside.

Cognitive behavioural therapy—a purblind psychology, to be sure, a psychology without a psyche; but, more than this, and even more risibily, it is a hypnotherapy without hypnosis.

You arrive home, having left your laptop at the office. So you cast around for a pen or pencil—nothing. Somehow, you've emptied your entire apartment of inscriptive devices. Left without any means of working, of marking a difference, you engage in the central passion of contemporary life: you snack.

Derrida as educator.

Time to admit it, theorists: a central task of poetry is the continual re-creation of the meaning of love, and the reaffirmation of its significance.

The possible is the lead in the waterways of the human mind.

With the aim of comprehending our amusing misery, we should avoid having recourse to Spinoza's three basic affects—*cupiditas*, *tristitia* and *laetitia*—and instead invoke the small set of elementary punctuation marks. Applications would include a means to categorise moral theories (Kant, nothing after the first full stop; Aristotle, all commas; Mill, proliferation of parentheses), and a way to speak of the lives of relationships (at the end of the second year, it seemed like we'd arrived at a full stop, but it turned out to be a semi-colon).

Linguistics is, properly understood, a subfield of magnetics. Near social degree zero, parti-cles lock together in random sequences of nonsense. As the density of social reality increases, linguistic units begin to exhibit the Hall effect: meaning emerges. But there is no need to go as far as these advanced points—you need only consider the estimable strength with which verbs attach themselves to pronouns.

Cantilevering is a fine technology, deserving of a much wider application than bridges and art deco staircases. The cantilevering of desire seems to show particular promise—as a way of avoiding the two extremes of calcifying boredom and self-immolation.

The self-appellation 'Aussie' is entirely correct for citizens of a country pleased and proud of its diminutive secondary status, an 'also' to the rest of the world.

The saying goes that you can choose your friends but not your family—another piece of trite pap. Your biological family is the primeval swamp, the caul, out of which a second family grows, an illegally constituted entity, an under-the-table family. The gap between this second family and the first is one of the more reliable measures of moral progress.

To reform yourself is hard, admittedly. But it pales into insignificance in comparison with the effort required to reform your view of someone else, perhaps the most difficult thing to do as a human being—with the exception of reforming your view of yourself.

All of Sartre is to be found in his lie about the greatness of the Soviet Union—in the name of *public relations*.

Worst side effect of prolonged exposure to your family: it breeds an incapacity to dislike anything honestly, above all in their company.

Leaving aside the ubiquitous pidgin it forms with speech and gesture, silence is a language of its own and on its own terms, with its own grammar, its own metaphors, its own social conventions—and its own silences.

Hypocorism, the signal trait of the Australian mind.

Art galleries are tracts of hostile wilderness, visited by unwitting hordes of tourists on reckless safaris they arrive unprepared for ... no telling when the predators inhabiting these spaces will turn from indifferently grazing on the near-imperceptible attention they are given and towards acts of terrible violence.

Emoticons — those little creatures that feed on the excrement of hegemony. Note their ease in their native environment, the trough of risible swill we amusingly call 'social media', a phrase that distinguishes itself by being both a pleonasm and an oxymoron at the same time.

The strange contemporary desire to rid education of its violence, to demarcate every sharp object in advance ... a paradoxical endeavour, given that education is just the name for *spiritual flensing*.

Sigmund Freud. If he had not lived, we would have had to create him. And so we did — in just the way he predicted!

Paterson is right: the sestina is odious, trivialising, boorish. It also happens to be the poetic form closest to spontaneous human speech, whose excessive fixation with and repetition of a few words, its incapacity to come to grips with novelty, and its sickening obsession with colouring between the lines are its hallmark characteristics.

Feng shui: monetised Gestalt.

The amusing fiction of the photographic instant. Perhaps it's a story we tell ourselves to avoid thinking about what might really be hidden down there in the smallest cracks of time — likely horrors so unbearable that they make Lovecraft's lucid nightmares seem like the charming sketches of a placid and absent-minded amateur botanist.

Shanghai conveys the overwhelming impression that it is the city that keeps up with time itself. But it is also the proof that time breaks open everything, hence its importance as philosophical exemplar.

Creation, reason, violence: neither the first nor the second without the third, though the second strives to purify itself from the first. Profane ground of history.

The depressing, manic contemporary search for correct pronouns ... what a perverse hunger, this hunger to make ourselves easy targets.

Subpuncting, likely the antecedent of ellipsis, is due a return to the cosmos of our self-understanding. After all, what is more to the point regarding human nature than the fact that we obscure as much as we say whenever we speak?

The tyranny of the orgasm, whose force as law is exercised at all times, above all when it is not imminent. Could it be that the pleasure we garner from this alleged priapus of sex is the pleasure of being purely and simply in accordance with the rule of law?

MATERIALIST DOMESTIC

Since, therefore, the soul is the gearbox of the
    body
I spend the morning grinding on the stick
To shut out its hoarse mewing.

Worse by far: the noise your jaw makes
Whenever you are chewing.

III

To look into a mirror is to gaze into the past—and not your own.

Our profligate eisoptromania. At least we possess a passing adequate therapeutic treatment: psycho-analysis, the science of the mirror.

Everything grew heavier with suffering and disgust. The world, already overladen, began to slowly implode, becoming smaller, denser. Soon, it was reduced to a single woman, staring with horror at the back of her head in a mirror no bigger than her own face.

Taking every image as a mirror—this is the greatest of modern manias, the hunger for high-fidelity representation. We mistake ourselves if we think this is a purely technological phenomenon, since its animus is that dark spiral, itself without double, that draws us ever into the destruction of difference. Our Narcissus wanders interminably, in search of a watercourse deep enough to drown in. The search is fruitless, for every river and stream, every screen and mirror, is unfaithful, and will refuse to reflect our own fantasies alone.

Her fascination with Instagram soon became a fixation, a perverse hunger. You left her—how could you not? The only thing she desired any more was to prematurely replace every person in the world with their own chalk outlines.

Picasso's *La Baignade*. It's easy to imagine someone seeing the image, especially those small worried faces, as a lazy joke. In truth, though, the face on the horizon, especially its scale, could be anything at all. It exists only to make the horror of the horizon itself rise up.

The universal mediatisation of human experience has forever destroyed any justification of the beliefs in human goodness, kindness and the progress supposedly implicated in history. The background murmur we used to take as the whisper of untold millions finding joy has been amplified nearly beyond bearing, and we hear it now as what it is — the twisting and howling of the spirit.

Consider the fact of blinking. It is sight and none of the other senses that the body periodically interrupts, and this is to stop it from tending towards the horizon behind everything it is currently examining. Correlate: your hands are masks and cenotaphs; their main function is not to grip or use but to direct your vision towards what's right in front of you.

What to make of this ubiquitous desire in activist circles, not to mention in the whole phantasmagoria of the news media, for transparency? It is difficult to avoid the conclusion that there is a quite non-communal, non-political drive at the root of all of this, a kind of obsessive, charged scopophilia: the desire is a desire to *expose*. As if this wasn't perverse enough, our 'leakers' are praised for *exposing others*. Like all good pornography, leakers' manifestos allure because through them we can feel violent termination by proxy.

The crestfallen guffaw that arises in you every time you consider that the tale of Narcissus is allegedly told from the point of view of the 'real' man, and not that of the reflection. The tale has never really been understood. Anyone who spends a long time looking in the mirror ends up, not drowned in their own image, but *submerged in the world*.

Go ahead, snort the tain. You'll encounter the other, and the counter to the animal kingdom, instead, where the law of camouflage reigns.

Representation — the shadow human existence casts in language.

The mirror is not just one class of technologies, but their root, their kernel. And to say that its effect is fundamentally derived from society is no objection to this. The mirror is the first and final socio-technical device. Even that hyphen is a mirror.

The ignorance of the mirror to the passage of time, in its flagrant promotion of the lie of eternity. It's like a friend that tells you 'Looking good, man!' at each moment — except that we believe it.

T.: 'Nobody had ever seen me with such clarity, just as I am. I miss being seen, *really seen* by her.' 'You're lucky you broke things off when you did. What kind of cruel lover would plunge you even *deeper* into the visible?' Helping someone disappear to themselves is the fundamental act of foreplay; kindness consists in rendering the ones we love as imperceptible as possible.

The person we see in the mirror is always and *a priori* a liar.

You should be wary never to let the experience of suffering convince you that sustained happiness— its luminous twin—is possible. Indeed, one of suffering's main lessons is that there are no twins.

Visibility is the matrix of perversion, sight the precursor of sin. A perverse deity, the one who insisted on *showing* them the apple.

The technology closest to the mirror? The Dutch toilet, whose distinctive design aims primarily not for the ablution but the inspection of shit.

The most common of our baser impulses is perhaps neither apathy, nor selfishness. It is the unreflective desire to punish the ones that appear to care about you—because they *appear* to care about you.

You find yourself wondering what it would be like to have an eye on either side of your head. It would be a relief to not have to see things twice and from two slightly different points of view — or, at least, to be able to decide not to.

Every fantasy is finally the fantasy of and for an intermediary.

IV

Philosophy is extremely difficult; poetry, merely impossible. This explains the late-blooming character of the philosopher observed by Socrates, but also the perennial swarms of amateur adolescent poets — adolescence being the season of the complete misrecognition of negative prepositions.

The clearest evidence that you are in the presence of a philosopher? Their impatience with even the slightest invocation of the relative.

Hegel's *Phenomenology of Spirit* — the overwrought tale of what it's like to wake up with a raging, bilious hangover on the day of a large writing deadline that you nevertheless meet.

Hypotheticals are the Prozac of the masses.

Most academic philosophers are parasites on philosophy. Content drinking philosophy's *leche de tigre*, they subject it to exactly — no more, at least — the kind of scrutiny given to the narrative undulations in the canons of superheroes by comic book collectors. They are aficionados, not thinkers.

You'll settle for etymology being wrongly conceived of as an analogue of philosophy, if it rules out any disastrous confusion of it with philosophy itself.

The Liar's Paradox ... what a trifle. Try uttering the words 'I want to die' if you want to watch the logicians scurry.

Apocalypse is a psychopathological rather than a cosmological category. The lover on the cusp of abandonment, real or imaginary, is the apocalypt in their native state. The doomsayer, correlatively, is just a particularly megalomaniacal lover, anxious at the thought of being jilted by even the smallest feature of their world.

The fact of distraction undermines every recourse to method.

One of the pacts made by the alcoholic involves the exchange of memory for solace, which is to say the choice to cope with the present at the cost of enervating the past and thereby attenuating the feeling of the future's spectral gaze. The rule is a simple one: spend all of yesterday's pay cheque today in order to bankrupt and belittle the future. Thereby the wound of time may be partly cauterised.

What is the strange feeling that arises in you when it becomes clear that your lover thinks more about sex than you do? Is it ... *gratitude*?

Here's an enigmatic Sunday morning scene: in an empty car park, a hastily discarded condom wrapper, nearby the condom, still bloated with its first and final meal, neatly tied off. Carelessness and care, always — whatever our tedious moralising might tell us — run in that order. Think of all of the things that would never have eventuated had we proceeded the other way around, starting with the condom itself.

Whenever the last light goes out — and there will be a last light, and it will go out — there will be a last thought, which will be not be remarkable for being the last.

In the bewildering trenches of the everyday is where love appears just as it is: an irredeemable mess. This is a lesson for those who labour under the heading of *philosophia*, since love does not bring wisdom and it is not wise to love. From this point of view, the love of wisdom shows itself for what it is: a peculiar wager against the everyday.

He finishes writing the book. Now there are two of them, in competition for who will be forgotten first — though only one of them is afraid of both outcomes.

We live in the age of health — and we are sick with it.

A journalist is asked why, given the looming threats to her life, she lives on, under duress and the threat of violence, in Mexico City. She answers: 'I have lost many things in my life...' But this is a reverie that distracts from the real answer: to find, for everyone else, *what is not here*.

Rigorous training for actors involves a progressive decomposition of natural posture, habituated ways of walking and standing, of holding things, of listening and looking. Philosophers should be trained in the same way, not metaphorically but literally, and the dirty habits of analogy and metaphor would be the first familiar animals to go under the knife.

Again, and surely not for the last time, you mistranslate *Es* as *ego* and *Ich* as *id* in a lecture on Freud. Even your unconscious conspires with Lacan.

The desire to know anybody too well should be carefully suppressed — not because people are in truth wretched (of course, of course) but because we are all each of us profoundly uninteresting, and it is impossible to love what is banal. Since nothing is interesting beyond a certain point, we should attend to the ethical character of the silhouette, the partial sketch, the hasty innuendo, the aphorism, the hint.

Einaudi and Mondadori both desired the same meal; they knew that to wrestle over it would be to spoil it; their notable solution was to trick the meal into thinking that the choice of predator was his own.

The name of Ted Hughes always elicits the same visceral response: you *coward*, you *coward*.

Arbus is completely right. The chiaroscuro of love must be maintained even in the act of its traversal, every intimate science. The ideal of honesty must be chained to its kennel.

When do you really have your *own* money? When you can buy drugs for your friends — that is, when you can afford to open an aperture on the inhuman for someone other than yourself without resorting to direct violence or an art gallery.

There is some requisite of mastery in philosophy, but it does not run to the core of what a philosopher does. They are not the masters of thought, but its perverts. In turn, a concept is not a model to be copied but a crack obsessively returned to, but not, in accordance with the ruinous confusion, a crack to be seen through.

The paradox of the poet's expression of their hunger for a 'we', for a primary, natal bond, in language. Language, what is most inhuman in human existence, resists absolutely — that is, with absolute duplicity — every attempt to treat it as the natural vector for its impossible obverse.

A WORD FROM OUR SPONSOR

I write this watching your house
slowly slip its hawsers and drift up
into the night air. From here I can
see into the kitchen from underneath,
finally a pristine and happy space,
our scuff marks and domestic disturbances
left on the ground as it bloats away,
the arsehole of the sink showing,
bleached clean and white.

Meanwhile, the pastoral is rotting,
the dithyramb is long since
in the arms of Hades,
and you've snorted its ashes
out of someone else's
Crack. God is truly dead, and you,
I surmise, among his final prank calls.
Your slight sundress hid an unexpected
Panoply, the whole redistricted contents
Of Pandora's lamentable box.

But tonight, I contemplate a last time
The one long borstal summer
We spent grinding on each other,
Industrial tools, blind and hard.
Reclined, the owl of Minerva smouldering
In my pipe, I'm watching your lofty kiss-off,
The low-wattage fireworks of your
stately drift into very early, very smug,
Obsolescence.

How pointless it is to complain (reflame the pipe
    again),
You think, as bad as any apology.
All of this will happen again
First the joy then the debasement.
But for now let's all enjoy
This commercial ad placement.

V

The child knows to be serious in her pleasure;
the adult becomes frivolous in his attempts at
profundity.

Beware of disbelieving too many lies at too great
a speed.

You are told to be kinder to yourself, that you
wouldn't treat your friends the way you treat
yourself. Yes, but those you count among your
friends are *better* than you.

'World' — a marketing term for Charon's ferry.

Of course, true love, seduction unblemished, grief
that rhymes with time, exist only in art. This fact
reflects not only the myopic reach of the imagination but art's place and power.

The only ethics that matters turns around you not
identifying with yourself. It is not I with whom I act
in accordance, but the other one who I will have
become.

Artificial intelligence: this pleonasm would be as
old-fashioned and amusing as the images of
catastrophe that it often summons, except for the
obvious fact that our own Apollonian genius has
done everything and more than these images
manifest. So let's not pretend that Skynet's

coming-to-consciousness would be anything more
than a merciful reprieve for humankind.

The sole problem with opinion is the ease with
which what is not opinion is mistaken for it.

Brecht's theatre is like an inside-out fortune
cookie: obscure and imperious, then bland.

The analogical is the mystical, misplaced.

Days like today, pen in hand but not pointed
anywhere in particular, you really don't know what
you're doing. Even if it's 'about' the same thing,
your teaching is a way of hiding your powerlessness from yourself.

There is an undeniable pleasure, and not a small
one, in easy answers to difficult questions — true
or not.

Close to unknown; nearly invisible; all but content-
less; an almost entirely transparent trickle of time.

In our race to affirm capacity, difference in ability
as different ability, we risk erasing the fact of
diminution. There is less just as there is more.
To hide this is to labour in the name of diminution
of thought, and to belittle the only source of
genuine affirmation.

Allegory: metaphor missing its object.

The pen can't reach out. It is good within a fraction of a centimetre of its point of application. All things have their own proper spacing, a lesson often worth recalling given our propensity to take one object as paradigmatic of others—the human body, for instance.

VI

One afternoon in bed, she compared with amusement the relative sizes of our ribcages. Excellent: another source of anxiety, seeded, as are all the others, in the soil of sex.

Having and wanting, together and alone, mingle in the shifting halo of human firelight. We cannot know the direction in which we move when we act.

The lover pits the beloved against the world. No wonder it always, sooner or later, turns out the way it does—with an 'accident'.

'What's your secret fantasy?', she asks, and because I wanted her to act it out, I was drawn into describing it. But in doing so, of course, the fantasy passed out of our grasp. A fantasy is not spoken, or even thought, but *felt*, and the moment language gets hold of it, it's done. She may as well have asked me to bring her to orgasm solely by recounting Euclid's postulates.

She was right, I had used her, but not in the way she thought—her body had been wedging open the door of sanity for me.

No act could better express your excessive self-certainty. And now you are free of the plague of my doubts.

In the beginning, we had this agreement: no sleeping with other people without talking to each other about it first. These days, we sleep around for something to talk about.

I spent an afternoon seducing her, slowly, taking care with all the details. That body, holding a fork, leaning sideways in her dress, idly tapping her foot, is now disrobing, hot and smooth and wet with sweat and all the rest. But at some point, as we fuck, it all changes. I find, suddenly, that what I really desire is for the tape of time, hiccuping along its spool, to reverse and replay, as I become the axis of its rotation, reliving the perfect moments of anticipation, acquiescence and revelation that now lay in the rear-view mirror. If there was a heaven, it would be this—the ongoing, all-consuming delight in seduction without any consummation.

What drove me back to see her again? To find certitude in my attraction? Or justification for my adjacent self-disgust?

To ruin everything, to disappoint everyone else, to have no interiority, no secrecy left that would shelter our disaster from each other's eyes—it was this that we had wanted, and once had. But the irruption of mere happiness was our ruin.

The promise of your laughter, your easy shifting contour barely muttering in the dim light, my hope that tomorrow the molten, witty part of you would rise up from the flammable dross of your heavy stupidity, your victimised self-obsession, your hangman's sympathies ... one day we were in bed, you knocked over the candles and I just let them burn.

Her use of my full name—enough all by itself to bind me to the mandrake root.

R.: A fragile swarm of desires without an apiarist. With me and my smoke out of her way, she'll find plenty of allergy-prone proto-victims happy to blindly construct her a hive.

The moment we settled on private names for each other, we were done. Since then, I've been careful to stick with generic terms of adoration in order to protect the singularity of my lovers.

Bureaucracy is not defined by but obsessed with its limits.

She always advances *mirror first*.

Regarding Sunday afternoon: it'll be impossible to forget your delicate gestures, you in your red shift, calm centre amidst the maelstrom of the failures that seemed to be devouring me ... you, that teacup in a storm.

We navigated the danger of dishonesty without incident. But we did not see the more insidious threat now fraying our stitches, the threat of telling the truth at the *wrong speed*.

She and I: the one, too much wick; the other, too much wax.

The sex was only good because we shared the same analyst, someone who knew exactly at what distance and at which angle to hold the mirror.

Instead of cursing her, I suppose I should have thanked her. The massive transfusion of disdain she administered killed many soft and weak things in me that I would have later taken, catastrophically, to be hard and strong.

This last, most flagrant act of infidelity, the last time she and I would fuck in her rehearsal room, finally gave me the certitude I had long sought: I was Narcissus jacking off into a shallow, dirty stream.

Because she doesn't know how pitiful the proportion of my effort deserves to be thought of as effort, she thinks my work is all equally heroic — and therefore all equally pitiful.

Next time you think you're in the flush of new love, she said, get her to piss on your palm. And pay attention to the speed at which it cools.

In my cowardice, I was relieved — too relieved, really — that she ended it. She had finally seen what had been clear to me from the start: that her very real love for me could make no room for my equally real self-hatred.

Her handwriting became so wild, reckless and illegible, she seemed possessed. The marks were no longer words, but the literal description of a struggle, as if her soul, dipped in ink, was staggering around the page. Her life itself had made it impossible for her to write her name.

You had promised to *drown me more often*. But these days, you're always saving me, pulling me back up into the air and the light. This may be where life is found, but exposing me to this much of it will only bring about our mutual death all the more quickly.

The way she went red, on her face, her neck, her chest, when she was turned on ... in the end, I fucked her just so that I could witness the unearthly beauty of her blushing. No longer a person, or even a name, but a shade.

To this day, I cannot decide if her promises were the web, the spider, or the dead husks of flies.

Our relationship worked just as long as an expired phone card — the moment you answered my call, it was over.

VII

Every word in a poem must be earned. Rhyme is how poets bribe themselves and their readers into a bargain.

Starve hunger.

The farcical image of a nurturing Mother Nature ... even mangoes contain trace amounts of kerosene.

La Rochefoucauld rightly notes that the customary means for defending ourselves from the fact of death do not withstand close scrutiny. The same is true of his aphorisms. Their 'noble' origins and court concerns might appear mere gilding on a first pass, but, the closer one reads, the more it seems that there is nothing but gilding here. We are left looking at ourselves in the woozy mirror of an aristocrat's leisure.

The idea of judging without guilt is a fantasy of the Left that must be abandoned. It is only by embracing the violence of pluralism and pluralism *at the same time* that the weakling democracy can survive.

Poems, rafts of driftwood.

In the ideal world, nature would have precluded the advent of either the plant *or* the animal. Such profligacy ... as with all spendthrifts, you end up asking yourself: *what does nature have to hide?*

There are no examples, only viscid secretions of prejudice that threaten the agility of thought.

An aphorism is not a reflection. It makes of a mirror's shard a weapon.

All real writers strive to create, even if only *inter alia*, a new grammatical person.

A lecturer giving a successful class is perhaps the closest a human being comes to a python unhinging its jaw.

Brand of Chinese wine: Terroir; brand of Chinese vodka: Kafka. Same category error.

The entirety of politics consists solely in the variable intertining of Hume's fork.

Sun Tzu's *The Art of War*: often read as a treatise on the psychology of the master. Little attention is paid to the fact that it is for the most part a discussion of kinds of territory, less again to the kind of territory constituted by *The Art of War* itself.

Catalogue the arsenal of new weapons created every day in speech.

An impasse is not the end of thinking, but an

invitation to suspend and examine an apparent mastery.

Consciousness: a vampire that feeds on itself. No — too dramatic. The *self-licking icecream*.

THE BIG REVEAL

Temporarily distracted in her satiety
She spat the oil of her hair back onto the bed
And drew, slow and steady down the length of my
    sternum
A rakish coastline in my blood. Then, warming to
    the task

Murmured in my ear 'Time to see what you've been
    hiding'
First one finger, then three, went into the new slot
She dug ever deeper, and was halfway through the
    mattress
Before the realisation pulled her up.

VIII

The aphorist writes as an eccentric in their own language and culture. To be too much of a place and a time is to cede the difficult realm which engenders them. At the same time, there is no aphorism that is not aimed at some such present. Aphorisms can only be stumbled into (not onto); their writer is at home in the world to which they are addressed, but *clumsily*.

The automat imitates that from which the idiomat deviates. Our beliefs in freedom and self-determination are pernicious and stubborn parasites on freedom itself.

To become nothing more than a bruise handed from lover to lover...

Nothing about infidelity is troubling, other than the experience, and its anticipation, of being caught. Roussel was right: everything involved in love should be kept secret, behind closed doors or at least submerged in the anonymous flux of the city—not because it is morally suspect, but because without secrecy it comes to absolutely nothing.

Lists, like analogies, are the philosopher's syphilitic rashes, pointless exercises in mastery, and placeholders for thought that will never be undertaken.

Aphorisms arise in the course of the immediate friction of language with reality. Aphoristic writing is therefore, despite a certain appearance, one of science's broodmates, confirming that one can indeed gain purchase on reality, *even out of the corner of one's eye*.

Aphorisms are in no way anecdotes, but rather tools for preventing the reduction of experience to anecdotes.

Seduction is a formal art—hence the relative unimportance of what is said.

The relative flatness of England is what made 'England' possible. Hard to say what makes it possible now.

Rule of thumb: keep the number of opinions and arseholes alike down to the strict minimum.

Nationalism, the fatal lure for so many poets, is the disastrous confusion of the canvas for the model, the ground meat for the meal.

Aphorisms must not be confused with propositions that *merely* profound in character. The ambition of being superficial and profound at once is what distinguishes the aphorism from the fulgurating host of its contemporary rivals which, due to their stabs at unalloyed profundity, are immediately assimilated. They slip easily down the lubricated gullet of stupidity, which knows that the way to eat such morsels without incident is to simply avoid chewing, all the better to immediately begin regurgitating them in the form of commentary.

Words are always written on someone else's back. Eye contact and writing are mutually exclusive. If someone looks you in the eye while writing, you can be sure that your workday is over and a seduction is underway — though it may be their attempt at the seduction of thinking. Try to avoid confusing these two.

Borges has taught us that one should not see and then write, but write in order to see. It should go without saying that his blindness has nothing to do with this.

The writing of poetry produces a healthier state of mind than the writing of philosophy — sharper, kinder, more honest. When writing aphorisms, though, you simply cease to exist. And the aphorist also learns which of the two is preferable.

An aphorism must bear weight. In its brevity and directness, it strives towards the fulcrum, aims to occupy the load-bearing point of the materials it summons. This point is *often* what its use of italics indicates.

Language demands nothing, wants nothing, says nothing. Its single proper capacity, fully exercised at every moment, is to silently wait.

Eating and drinking present themselves, front up to you, as the prerequisites of writing and thinking—a classic con. What they really signify is the end of all meaningful activity. The suppressed premise of this argument is simple: 'the future is just a dimension of the present'.

There is no writing at the heart of thinking. The archer's eye trains, not on the arrow, but the target.

The aphoristic form makes only two demands: honesty and daring; great aphorisms result when these demands conflict.

It's the world itself that's stuck in our throats—how can we keep writing?

Whitman: 'The proof of a poet is that his country absorbs him as affectionately as he absorbed it.' God's bodykins, man! The proximity to vacuity shows us what Father Whitman is worth to thought (next to nothing); it also tells us something about thinking and its attendant dangers, and what offends here is the alliance of optimism and stupidity. Nevertheless, poets should embrace this sentiment ironically, an absolute hostility to the claims made by and on behalf of country and every other form of patronymy being its essential animus. They should also embrace it satirically—after all, one proof of a poet is the ease with which they may take themselves to be fuel for a fire.

The value of an aphorism lies in the number of

points of view it affords. A good aphorism is a house with one door but many windows.

Writing poetry is like flying a kite: the occasional moments of lift only punctuate the feeling of being completely fucking inept, lacking any of the relevant skills, and looking utterly ridiculous to your friends into the bargain. And if you somehow succeed, there's never any escaping the feeling that it had little or nothing to do with you. (And, dear reader, if you compose verse and do not recognise yourself in this portrait, it is time to *look away from the mirror*.)

IX

Language 'possession' has driven us ever deeper into the stupefying dumbness of the animal.

Seduction: from one point of view, programme, from another, narrative. But its consummation is marked by the achievement of their indiscernibility.

You tell a series of easy lies to protect the minimal stability the erratic course of your life possesses. But precisely because it is erratic, deranged, the ensemble of lies appears equally deranged — a certain negative image of the absolute uncertainty that presents a perfect description.

To write well truly is to become part demon — that is, less human. The time of the book, the body of the book, the destiny of the book, all of these are entirely foreign to human beings. The writer trades, a page at a time, her place in the human race.

Stanza is another name for obsession.

Delacroix didn't put the point strongly enough: all lines are monsters. It's hard to imagine anything more wild, more terrifying. No wonder textbooks that address the physics of surfaces begin with the fiction of an absolute volume. The line only appears, muzzled and in third place, as a convenient abstraction, a comforting revisionism.

Writing and thinking, locked together around an essential powerlessness. But while the incapacity of thought to effect anything appears in the wake of its act, writing's impossibility is the first thing about it that you encounter.

Philosophy is not the discourse of the master, whatever certain *maîtres à penser* would tell us. Granted, it is the discourse of megalomaniacs, but a megalomania *without narcissism*.

An ex-lover with a penchant for prediction once told you that, the next day, you would see the three most beautiful women you had ever seen. After working for the morning at the abyssal task of the translator, you walked around aimlessly, passing the afternoon traversing a fractal path through the city. You did not see the three most beautiful women you had ever seen.

But deep in the night, the awful possibility suggested itself: you did not know, had never known, what beauty is. It was years before you isolated the shrapnel in you, and understood what she had done.

Deconstruction—the finest and best flower of neurosis, but one that takes altogether too long to wither and die, casting a shadow that kills too many other new things in the flush of their youth.

Consciousness is to thought what leprosy is to the body—except that no cure for the former is in sight, only palliatives with pernicious side effects.

A major reason for being a drunk is profound boredom. (Let's see the government's health apparatchiks deal with that one.)

Experiment: try to stop yourself from falling asleep for *no reason*.

The imperative of love is to *modify gravity*: the weight of bodies, the conditions of their impact, the nature of their mutual attraction, all of this must be made new. Nobody ever falls in love, only ever out of it.

Fantasy—subcutaneous fat of the self; skin of the social.

Noblesse oblige? Perhaps. Despite its protestant prestige, however, obligation does little more than sour the soul.

M. tells you, probably in an attempt at consolation, that, since infidelity is inevitable, we need to learn to talk and think about it as little as possible. Sage words—but for the fact that in becoming an object of speech at all, even in the context of this very conversation, the current infidelity and the faith with which it breaks is the catalyst for the next unfaithful act. For the promise of the overcoming of infidelity is itself one part of seduction. A couple sleeps not in a bed, but on an ever-shifting surface of promises and lies.

Yesterday, the inveterate C. tells you that to write is

to live without life. You almost had to bite your tongue to not immediately reply: And?

Compare thinking without writing, and writing without thinking. And now compare being unable to write with being unable to think.

Drinking will doubtless bury you, but you will never renounce it or its ability to reveal the proximity of the accident.

Artaud's lesson is in need of perennial renewal: we must defend and deploy the concept of cruelty, above all against morality.

The starched moralists. You would call them simpletons, but for the fact that it is clearly the simplest things that they cannot comprehend, beginning with the fact that *debauchery is its own reward*.

Why drink? To stop the moment from breaking back down into its component parts, namely what a thing is and what it could have been.

What used to be called sentimental education more or less boils down to a lesson about sight: never look directly at the horizon.

THE ROPE KITE

Around that flaxen ourobouros
I carefully run my gaze, twice, three times
Not quite a perfect circle
But the more alluring for its eccentricity.
Eye and mind both fit it snugly
At least from the right distance.

This thing I had tied myself
I mean, by myself and for myself
Hangs next to me in this small room
A terrible force looming over a thin shadow
A mute premonition of consequence
And stiller than any conviction.

That shadow can seem the opening
Gambit of an illuminated manuscript
But the thing itself may appear as
A ladder, an empty storeroom, a bridge
Or the long and lonely rope wrist of an anchor
Lost in seas too heavy for it.

But tilt your head and you may see it aright
It's the bare frame of a kite hung upside-down
The skeleton of a beast of flight
The embryo of every escape
True, not many ever see it this way
Make one yourself and you will.

The rope kite, like its brethren
Belongs to earth as well as air,

Is one means of reconciling this broken couple
Like them, it is at its stillest
Before it takes off, while it waits,
And at the apex of its flight. Between, it trembles.

Some days, I long for it to catch me up
And throw me joyously into the sky
To punch the wind out of my weak lungs.
On others, for its one strong arm
To hold me firm and calm near cold soil
To pack night into my bent bones.

Mostly, though, I simply entertain
Its slim silhouette out of the corner of the eye.
All my hours hang, like the kite,
Between atmosphere and earth
My interregnal friction not yet charged enough
To set that rope machine to work.

X

Some nights, whatever your philosophical predilections, Plotinus seems completely correct: 'Eternity on one side, psychological time on the other, and nothing between the two.' Or, as he should have put it: there is nothing halfway between sex and nothing.

Freud's hypothesis of the latency period is the greatest extant justification of leisure: what else is it, after all, than a holiday from death? The first decisive critics of leisure, on the other hand, are goth teens, whose disdain for everyone else arises due to their (correct) sense that we're all effectively dead already. What is called Cotard's Syndrome is simply the manifestation of this truth—less a syndrome than an open secret that we conspire to hide inside the body.

To pity is always to pity a myope—and, alas, to be one.

Self-hatred is a halting affair. Whenever one of your failings confronts you, time pauses as it slaps you up around the chops, exposed again to this one or another of your moral pockmarks. A staggering descent, as if down an uneven spiral staircase. Narcissism, on the other hand, is an intoxication of remarkable smoothness and timelessness. The smoothness it shares with the mirror; the timelessness, with death.

The value in learning history is to be done with it. Behind its mildewing veil, learn to glimpse the abyss of time.

Little-acknowledged centrality of the city for politics. The *world* has been lyingly added.

The overripe odour of nationalism—detect even a hint and you can be sure you find yourself in altogether the wrong company.

The most venal of Australia's many sins is to have held up the animal in the human as the exemplar of the good life. All of its famed 'virtues' (mateship, barbeques) announce a preference for the simplest and most boorish bodily pleasures. The animals on the national crest were wisely chosen: a bird with a huge body and a tiny head, and an equally pea-brained marsupial with a built-in carry bag.

The degree of someone's stupidity will quickly become apparent when they begin eating. *What* we eat is merely a moral question; *how* we eat is what gives us away.

The most advanced mechanisms in Western society are given over to the task, at which they excel, of extracting spectres of the exceptional from the banal: for instance, the category of body dysmorphia.

Melancholy can be neither cured nor killed, but must be left to rot enough for it to fertilise new growth.

Time teaches contradiction: act quickly, with reticence.

The only surface we ever really write on are others' bodies. All other surfaces are intermedial, temperature-sensitive or waxen means of transmission, interregnal membranes that stand temporarily between one body and another.

Our excuses. We think the human spirit curdles in poverty, lack, want—but, make no mistake, what we call the human spirit is the curdling agent itself.

Every new lover destroys, in an instantaneous conflagration, all the others. At first, there is only a feeling of triumph and superiority. But then comes the realisation that the living body beside you will be prey to the horde of undead women that are already beginning rise up from their mingled ashes.

'In your hunger, you want things too soon, before their time.'— 'Not at all. The "too soon" does not exist, only the "too much" or the "too late".'

The purveyors of the Singularity (just one?), the fantasy of the end of death, and the subsequent spiritual triumph of the petit bourgeoisie ... never has the admonition 'be careful what you wish for' seemed more *apropos*. There is only one state in which the traumas involved in death and dying are absent, and that is the state of death itself.

The saving grace of human existence is the fact that we are not all stupid in exactly the same way.

A career in academia—a slow (?) death from anaphoric schlock.

In truth, desire is disembodied and disembodying. My desire to touch her on the neck is the desire to do so without using my body.

Suicide is surely the fundamental question of morality, *if it is a moral question*. In any case, it is not a philosophical question. The fact of death confronts us with innumerable problems, most of which are sublimated, a cello line in a busy piece. Suicide itself neither poses nor resolves any problem: it only postpones them forever.

The best thing you can be hopeful for in a lover's face after sex is serene indifference. Loathing, of course, is a horror, but so too are happiness and contentment—in these, it is too easy to see the reflection of other lovers. Only her indifference tells you that there is nothing more left to see.

Las Vegas. The fluid in the spine of humanity.

You read for one reason alone: to feel the pressure of your finitude, that is, to gain a presentiment of your current limits.

The task of philosophy, at least for some of its originators, was to teach the lesson of how to die. But this lesson is rarely well-learnt, above all because of the breaks most of its students must take due to the manifold illnesses that they suffer while in training. Even the contemplation of dying seems to involve the evacuation of the reality of living — that is, *sickness* — in order to engender an empty image of life against which to contrast a specular death.

That hope is the remedy for despair in the popular imaginary does not make the two the eternal halves of a diametrically opposed couple. They are not warring gods, but troubled siblings in a broken family. Hope, monomaniac, stays on the porch after the lamps are snuffed, while despair connives, foments a cult with the others. Despair needs hope angry, off-balance, reeling; hope forgets the existence of the others in the evangelical fervour that aims to transmute despair into kerosene for the next night's flame. But it is from hope's hair that the wicks are fashioned.

Nostalgic partisans of false, unfulfilled and unfillable past promises, bigots would deserve our pity, except that they first deserve *absolute* denegation, rendering any other response moot.

Amateur nihilist, *brunch decadent*, she was only up to a revolution in pronouns.

Weapons punch their victims back into a past without exit, empty the present of their presence. Strictly speaking, they do not have death as their *telos*. They aim instead at the creation of a world in which their victims would only ever *have* lived.

Anxiety: cut-rate post-traumatic stress disorder, lacking both stress and trauma.

You may sometimes think that it's envy, that you envy those who can so easily accept the stupidity of the world, the mortal blows it metes out according to its unpredictable schedule. But in truth, the tain behind this envy of yours is a feeling of superiority, all the more potent for never appearing in its own guise.

Every philosophy is a teratology written backwards.

People emote downcast about dying alone. They haven't thought the thing through: everyone should hope for such grace.

If human beings were more courageous, psycho-analysis would be more like witchcraft—and vice versa.

The shadow of a tool marks the limit of its misuse, just as does the shadow of a word.

All the cruel things that nest in childhood bodies ... The pupae develop unnoticed and, at the moment of their hatching, reveal themselves to be the implacable vectors of time itself.

XI

Cigarettes, those unsung little exemplars of automation. Once a flame pulls the ripcord, they'll smoke themselves alone in peace — or at least in blithe indifference to their putative smoker.

The soul is easily starved through overfeeding.

The essence of the larded and over-lauded ideal of 'the good life' is the management of disappointment. The fact that our contemporary moral technicians hunger for it to be more than this is the very crest of their intellectual insipidity.

'However slowly, you're drinking yourself to death.' 'Yes, but everything leads to death. If you want to judge me, you'll have to be more specific.'

Seduction, in all of its permutations, is already encoded in advance in space. Each of your hungry glances shares a place with those of Heloïse and Abelard.

Desire: early-onset death.

The stars, our ultimate judiciary.

Desires always run in a straight line, carrying us from their inception to our ruin. The whole of human history is composed of their flight, and it is only our cross-eyed selves that see them as a

diverting morass. They are real, the right lines—
we are their clumsy, ephemeral, distracted children,
their pale sparks, their darkening halos.

To properly love is to live in one's own death, to
inhabit the fact of your extinction. The dark-haired
woman at the end of the bar with the Welsh
accent—is she worth your life? Even if you choose
wrongly, that is the question that must be
answered.

The visible is to the sexual what the wave is to the
particle.

A temporal disproof *via negativa* of Stoicism—any
happiness or grief, boredom or anxiety projects
itself limitlessly towards the future. My current
happiness makes no room for any genuine consid-
eration of its absence. Affective life is a portrait in
serial monomania.

Ethics is a mastery of polyrhythm.

The suicide leaves only unanswered questions. But
this distinguishes him not at all from every other
person at every moment of their lives. Every note is
a suicide note in all but the final detail.

The larvae of sadness grow fat on the indigestible
husks of success.

Arguments against addiction reveal the limits of
our habits.

Frottaged to death by life.

The two sexes—one as it is, the other as it is imagined. But the truth is that the imaginary here is real, and the real imaginary—at least if the sex is any good.

Walking is, technically speaking, a specific form of falling.

It seems like your twenties, years spent labouring under the abject terror of death, are finally paying off—you seem to be becoming bored with the thought of dying. But now comes the fear: if you can become bored of even this, what could fall out of favour next?

Extend the narrative of a crime novel out endlessly, such that the pursuit and examination of suspects never concludes, and it begins to descend from fiction into fact. The crime novel tends, asymptotically, towards the telling of human history.

Nothing kills a relationship quicker than the demand to reveal all our secrets. This is what explains the suffering of love, whose pleasure in confession leads inexorably towards jealousy, itself another name for the absolute double bind forced on us by transparency. We have Proust because we cannot manage to keep our mouths shut. *Quod ergo demonstrandum.*

'Intelligent' cars, which watch in every direction for the event, are now beginning to be produced. In the future, they will be able to see kilometres and years into the future, as if Laplace's demon was your cab driver. When they do, driving will have finally lost the last of its charms, no longer sheltering any possibility for disaster.

The desire to be just one person in all circumstances is a telltale sign of an advanced progression of the wasting disease that stalks the land under the moniker 'truth'.

It is the politician, rather than the poet, who labours under the well-known edict to 'earn each word'. The poet's is: 'earn the right to the word's exploitation'.

We are nothing, and we come to nothing — *but in the gap how much love and pain there is.*

The spoon. What a concession to the oaf within us.

Imagine never having witnessed the happiness or grief, lust or repentance, of another person. Of course, this is an impossible exercise, and its very impossibility appears to demonstrate that we require precursor images of fundamental human states before we can have them ourselves — except, *ex hypothesi*, for the act of imagination itself.

You must have at least three lovers at any one time. Only two, and you'll find yourself circulating in the dull ochre over-trodden trenches of rivalry. Only one, and you'll sooner or later be back in the grip of the mirror.

In your endless battle with sex, there are no new fronts. Every time you encounter it, you find it facing away from you.

You can only look at a woman's breasts or her eyes at any one time. The propensity to look in one of these two directions, the relative strength of the two polarities, the speed of the transition between the two — all of these constitute the basic elements of a sexual optics. The way this gap and its correlates is managed in the visual register constitutes the kernel of gender relations *tout court*.

The hypochondriac's panic, shimmering like oil in an overheated pan, always contains a detectable allium trace of smugness. Unfortunately, it is better justified than almost any other human belief, which is why a hypochondriac so easily rejects imprecations to relax and put their anxieties in the proper context, to 'take it easy'. *My certainty that I'm going to die hovers in front of me every time I feel anything, but let me take a moment from my fear and trembling to tell you to shut the fuck up.*

The elementary effect of flattery is to temporarily make you forget that you are going to die.

The moment you're close enough to another person to find you need to choose which eye to look into, you've crossed a threshold; you can be certain that suffering is on the horizon.

Art's capacities include, let's not forget, the bringing of death to life — even the most clichéd B-movie bears this out. The variable mode of this apparition makes possible the distinction between comedy and tragedy. In the former, death appears as a necessary cameo, in the latter as a generalised opponent — in Sophocles, it is the messenger, in slapstick gravity.

People who are surprised — inevitably — at the suicide of someone they saw the very day before have failed to understand at least two absolutes of human existence.

History — the risible, ill-fitting prophylactic we never cease trying to slip over the perturbing anamorphic reality of Time.

The moral distaste that snoring engenders is easy to interpret as an affront to personal space, health and ease. But here as elsewhere the moral obscures the mortal. The snore is the noise made by the dead body hiding inside the living person — an *ante-mortem* death rattle.

You begin posing the questions of nihilism and suicide lightly, then fearfully, and finally *wistfully*.

The best that can be hoped for in your formative years are traumas of the right intensity and rhythm.

The only genuine palliative for the crushing fear of death is not the dream of another life but the presence of a second body.

Humanity — a sea of sirens without any sailors to seduce.

The earth we inhabit is an error, an incompetent parody. Mirrors and paternity are abominable because they multiply and affirm it.

Jorge Luis Borges

Seduce or Die
Jon Roffe

Design: Brad Haylock

First edition 2018
ISBN: 978-1-922099-29-7
Edition of 300

Typeset in STF Lido and FF Bau Pro families

Surpllus
PO Box 418
Flinders Lane 8009
Victoria, Australia

www.surpllus.com

Surpllus respectfully acknowledges the people of the Woi wurrung and Boon wurrung language groups of the eastern Kulin nations as the traditional owners of the unceded lands upon which the development of this volume has principally taken place.

Surpllus #27

JON ROFFE

Seduce or Die

Surpllus

Jon Roffe